For Mary, my dear stepmum,
who always keeps the light on for us.
K.T.

For Al, who knows about
these things. N.S.

Do Knights Take Naps?

Written by Kathy Tucker

Illustrated by Nick Sharratt

CAT'S Whiskers

THE WATTS PUBLISHING GROUP LTD

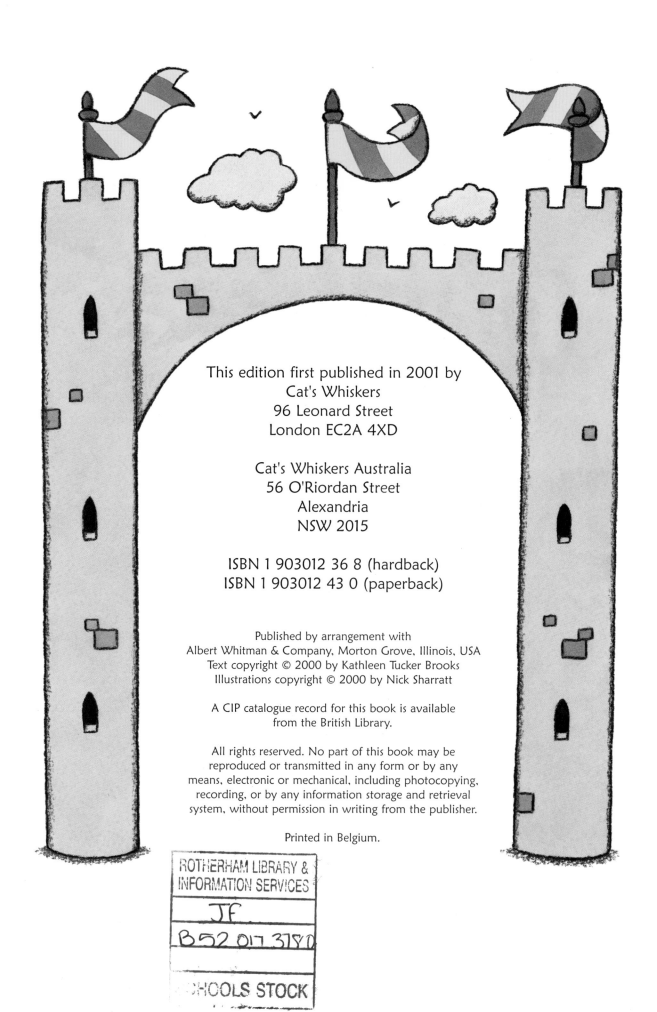

This edition first published in 2001 by
Cat's Whiskers
96 Leonard Street
London EC2A 4XD

Cat's Whiskers Australia
56 O'Riordan Street
Alexandria
NSW 2015

ISBN 1 903012 36 8 (hardback)
ISBN 1 903012 43 0 (paperback)

Published by arrangement with
Albert Whitman & Company, Morton Grove, Illinois, USA
Text copyright © 2000 by Kathleen Tucker Brooks
Illustrations copyright © 2000 by Nick Sharratt

A CIP catalogue record for this book is available
from the British Library.

Printed in Belgium.

What does a knight do?

He gets up before breakfast
and travels afar,
looking for people to save.
He fights the Bad Prince
and the Fiery Dragon
who lives in a cold, dark cave.

BAD PRINCE'S
CASTLE
5 MILES

FIERY DRAGON'S
CAVE
7 MILES

What does a knight wear?

Bright shiny armour
that clinks and clanks
and covers him head to toe.
He must lift his visor
and peek all around
to see which way to go.

What else does a knight need?

His very own shield,
a swishing sword,
a lance quite skinny and long,
a fearsome flail
with a ball and chain,
and a horse who's smart and strong.

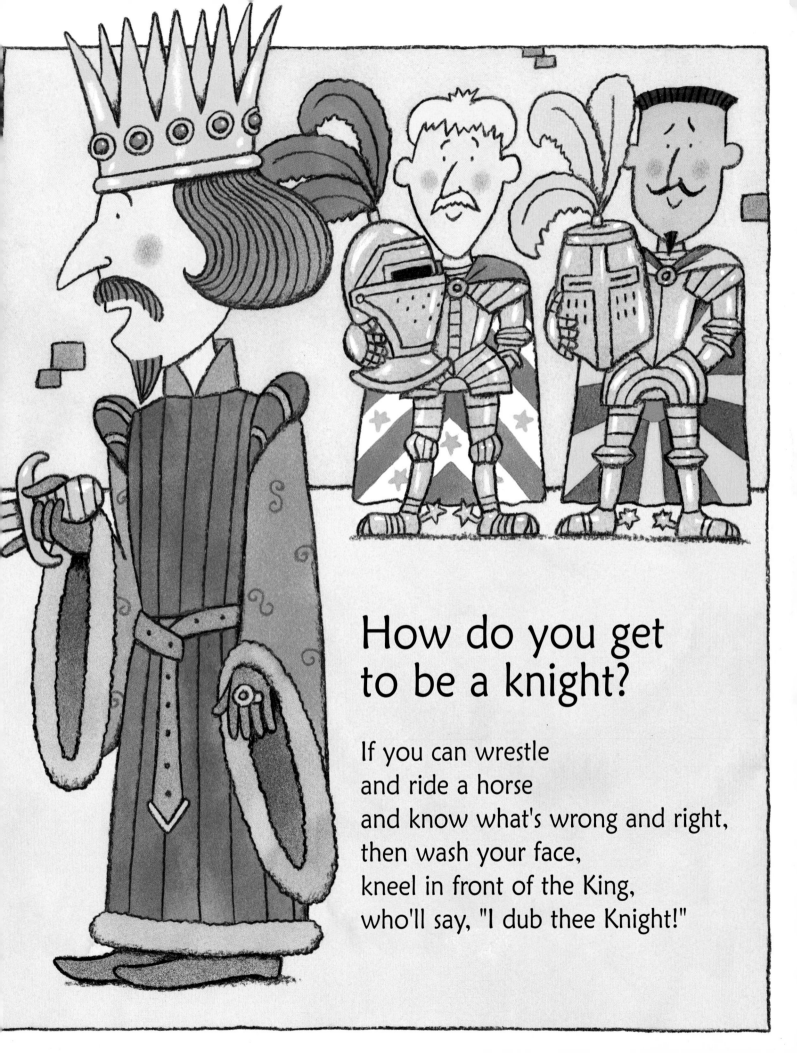

How do you get to be a knight?

If you can wrestle
and ride a horse
and know what's wrong and right,
then wash your face,
kneel in front of the King,
who'll say, "I dub thee Knight!"

Where do knights live?

They live in a castle
with towers upstairs
and secret rooms hidden inside.
A drawbridge that creaks
as it goes up and down
crosses the moat deep and wide.

SHHH!
DOOR TO SECRET
ROOM →

Do knights eat sweets?

No sweets at all,
only old apple juice
with chunks of salty meat;
some chewy brown bread,
and - if you're good -
there's honey as a treat.

What does the Bad Prince do?

To capture the castle,
he swims through the moat
and tries to climb the wall.
His men throw rocks
with a big catapult
and fire a cannon-ball!

How do the knights beat the Bad Prince?

They flash their swords
as fast as a blink
and chase the cowardly bunch.
That old Bad Prince
and his nasty men
soon run home for their lunch!

What does the Fiery Dragon do?

He roams the country
breathing flames
and causing a terrible scare.
He captures a boy,
and his little dog too,
roaring, "Stop me if you dare!"

How does the knight fight the dragon?

He grabs a bucket
and calls to the beast,
"Come out, don't be so mean!"
He tosses the water,
and the dragon's breath
turns into a cloud of steam!

Do knights have TV?

They don't have TV,
but they do have a jester,
who tells silly stories for fun.
He knows how to juggle
ten balls in the air
and catch them one by one.

What happens at a joust?

While everyone cheers,
the knights aim their lances
and ride their horses fast.
Each tries to knock
the other one off;
and the knight who falls is last.

What happens if a knight gets hurt?

He doesn't cry
if his knee is skinned
or he has a stomach-ache.
He puts on a plaster
and drinks up his juice,
then pauses for a break.

Do knights take naps?

Right after lunch
their mums tuck them in
and leave the light on in the hall.
They dream of their deeds
so brave and so good -
they're the very best knights of them all!

Good Knight!